TH
PERSPECTIVE
A Book of Inspiration

**Increase Your Child's Self-Esteem
by Helping Them to Discover a Peace Within**

I HOPE YOU ENJOY MY BOOK.

Mike Markovski

12-4-14

Mike Markovski
**Author, Consultant
Self-Esteem Coach**

The Peace Perspective
"Seeing the world in a new way"

 (586) 231-4277

 Mike Markovski

 m.markovski@comcast.net

thepeaceperspective.com

First Edition Design Publishing

The Peace Perspective
Copyright ©2014 Mike Markovski

ISBN 978-1622-875-47-4 PRINT
ISBN 978-1622-877-25-6 EBOOK

LCCN 2014933996

September 2014

Published and Distributed by
First Edition Design Publishing, Inc.
P.O. Box 20217, Sarasota, FL 34276-3217
www.firsteditiondesignpublishing.com

The Key To Open All Doors

*Raising our children to have inner peace
and love is what we need to do,
It is not an easy job but, as parents,
that peace must first come from you.*

*We must face life with a strong sense of peace,
By doing this, we will have a love
that will never cease.*

*Love once found dwells within us so deep,
We should not lock this love within us, but spread it
outwardly for others to keep.*

*Our essence, once uncovered, leads to a
life of inner peace and love,
The secret is that this essence comes from
both within and from above.*

*Once you discover your essence,
it will always be yours,
By believing in your own greatness,
you now have the key to open all doors!*

Mike Markovski

What does an author's name have to do with the writing of a book?

My given name foreshadowed my passion and eventual life direction. I was born in Macedonia and given the name Mire *(pronounced Me-ray)*. The name comes from the word *"mir"* which, in Macedonian, means *peace*. The pursuit of peace has been the main catalyst for the creation of this book. An interesting side note is that my Macedonian wife's name is Radojka or "Rada" for short. "Rada" means *happy* in Macedonian.

INTRODUCTION

What parent does not want to see their children have a life of inner peace and love? I believe inner peace and love is the greatest gift we can give our children. A peace within leads to a greater love of oneself and that love helps us to have a higher self-esteem. It is with this higher self-esteem that our children can best deal with the many challenges life has to offer. We all want to give our children the best chance for success in life, but what is the best way to make this success possible?

The Peace Perspective answers this question from a non-technical and unique personal perspective. This perspective maintains that when parents discover their own inner peace, they will then be more able to pass this important quality to their kids. The peace perspective approach consists of three central understandings. For individuals to reach the peace perspective, the following three questions must be answered:

➢ Who am I at my deepest level?
➢ What am I seeking in life?
➢ How am I going to achieve a more peaceful life?

We are all gifted with a spiritual essence that is the most powerful force in the universe. Our greatest need is not in finding happiness (external focus) but in finding a peace within (internal focus).

We achieve peace within by understanding the previous questions and disciplining our minds.

Knowing the answers to the previous questions is vital because it changes our perceptions of how we see our world. This new understanding will allow us to see life with a higher awareness (perception). A higher awareness will make our present moments more rewarding and cause us to make better life choices. We all can have a more peaceful life, but only, if we live life with a higher peace perspective.

Important topics discussed in The Peace Perspective:

- ➢ Why high self-esteem and peace are so important.
- ➢ Understanding why our peace perspective matters.
- ➢ How we can make our children feel more loved.
- ➢ Ways to reach inner peace.
- ➢ Techniques for helping our kids succeed.
- ➢ How the peace perspective can change society.

DEDICATION

To achieve anything worthwhile in life, we need the help of many loving people. In this regard, I have been very fortunate. Many people have contributed to my success to this point in my life.

I want to first thank my parents, Ilija and Ivanka Markovski, for their love and support. Throughout my life, they have taught me many valuable life lessons, which have helped me become the person that I am today.

In addition, I want to thank Violet Todorovski, Mark Kronner, and Nuran Shah for their many hours of reviewing the early editions of my book. They provided me with much useful insight and guidance. I also want to thank Tony Rubleski, author and marketing guru, for providing me with the encouragement to follow my passion and write this book.

My three sons, Daniel, Brandon, and Jason, were of much help in providing feedback in shaping this book to its final version. They were great kids, who now have become fine young men. My sons attended my self-esteem classes. Throughout the years, they have helped me develop the curriculum. They know, firsthand, the many topics discussed in this book.

Finally, I would like to thank the most important person in my life, my wife Rita (aka Radojka, Rada).

She has been so instrumental in helping me make this book, my lifelong passion, a reality. Over the years, her support has always remained constant and true. Her love has been the guiding force in my life. Thank you, Rita, my wife of 25 years, for making this book a reality. Always know you have been the source for making my world a much more peaceful and loving place.

PROLOGUE

A New Perspective

The need to provide our kids with a sense of inner peace has never been greater. Life, it seems, is moving faster than ever. This faster lifestyle places more demands on our children. With increasing demands can come stresses that need good, sound judgments. **Children with high self-esteem have good judgment and avoid negative consequences.** Unfortunately, far too many kids are not making good, sound decisions when facing life's challenges. By raising our kids' self-esteem, we can help to provide them with a new perspective so they can make better decisions.

Parents teaching their children to have inner peace and love is the focus of my book. **Life is all about choices. Children who have the gift of love see all the beauty in life and make wiser choices.** When our children have more love inside, they will have the means to handle life's challenges. Additionally, they will have the means to enjoy all the good life has to offer.

We will all experience in life both beautiful moments and challenging moments. There is a Chinese philosophy called Yin-Yang. The philosophy suggests that there is always an opposite to every quality in our world, such as good/bad, light/dark, happy/sad. To experience our world fully, we need to experience one side of a quality to appreciate the opposite experience. By teaching our kids to have an inner radiance of love and peace, they can learn to handle and appreciate the many experiences life has to offer.

Unfortunately, many children have a hard time handling some of their life challenges. Listed below are some sobering statistics. These statistics are the result of kids making bad decisions.

> In the next twenty-four hours, 1,439 teens will attempt suicide. [1]
> In the next twenty-four hours, 15,006 teens will use drugs for the first time. [1]
> In the next twenty-four hours, 2,795 teenage girls will become pregnant. [1]
> In the next twenty-four hours, 3,506 teens will run away. [1]
> Every seven minutes, a youth is arrested for a drug crime. [2]
> Every four minutes, a youth is arrested for an alcohol related crime. [2]

1. Source: Teen Help.
2. Source: Crime Time by Safe Place.

How My Self-Esteem Class Began

The story goes back to 1999, when my three sons were attending elementary school. I decided to join the elementary school parent advisory committee. Even back then, I believed in the importance of self-esteem. I requested, through the parent committee, for my sons' school to make some changes to their curriculum. I wanted a class to help the students achieve higher self-esteem. While at that time I was not an expert in self-esteem, I knew the value it held for our kids. Although I was not able to convince the group to make changes to the school's curriculum, the principal suggested that since I had a strong interest in the topic, I should develop my own self-esteem program.

My job at that time was as a full-time Controller at a construction company. I had no background for such an endeavor. What I did have was a strong need to make a difference in our kids' futures. I was a big believer in the power of positive thinking. The power of positive thinking had been an obsession of mine ever since I was a young man. I had read many books on this subject.

I put together a course description. My course plan was accepted. I began teaching the class, which I called *Self-Esteem: Creating Positive Results,* twice a year for four weeks. Each week, each session ran for 90 minutes. I decided to focus my work on kids in the 4th through 7th grades. I felt this was a critical age where kids' self-esteem is vulnerable. At this age, their self-esteem is more easily shaped. I have taught my class in the Metro Detroit area since 1999. The class size ranges between five and fifteen kids.

The Joy of Helping Children

Working with these kids over the years has turned out to be one of the most rewarding experiences in my life. The kids who first attend my class usually do not have any idea of what self-esteem is. The first question I ask the kids is why are they taking my class? Their answer usually is because their parents thought the class might be beneficial for them. This makes my job a little harder, knowing they are not there by their own choice. Surprisingly, in the final class evaluation, a vast majority of the students said they enjoyed the class.

Kids have a strong need to learn about self-esteem. Over the years, it has been amazing to see how excited the kids get about the class. The children love learning about the impact self-esteem can have in their lives. Several kids have even wanted to take the class again. Why did my students feel this way about my class? The class made the kids more aware of their own importance. Parents love their kids and try their best to make them feel important. It can also be beneficial for kids to hear they are special from people besides their parents. I see the spark these children get when I tell them how important they are. I explain how, with a deep belief in themselves, they can accomplish anything. If we can create a positive belief system within our kids, then they can more easily increase their feelings of importance. Over the years, I can just tell when the kids are getting my message. I am certain that something said in the classroom will someday make an impact in the students' lives.

While we cover many topics in my class, I have always held a central theme that is of the highest importance. **The idea conveyed to the kids, in many ways, is that we have the power of choice in any situation. While we sometimes cannot change the situation, we will always have a choice in how we react to the situation.**

My favorite example of this idea is the following: Suppose we have two kids, with equal ability, studying for a test. The first child reacts in a negative manner. He states the test is going to be very hard. He is certain he will fail. This negative energy makes this child not prepare properly. The child fills his head with doubt that leaves him with little confidence. The second child prepares properly and knows he will do his best. This makes him feel relaxed. He sees himself getting a good grade. This creates positive energy and a sense of calmness. Who do you think will do better on the test? The second child will do better on the test. He will also have significantly less stress.

Showing children they have options in any situation can be one of the greatest lessons they will ever learn. **<u>Teaching kids to recognize negative choices, and replace them with better choices, is one of the keys to a life of inner peace and love.</u>** It is a lot easier to change our reaction to a situation than to actually try changing the situation. We have to do a better job of conveying this knowledge to our kids. My hope is that this book, in some small way, will help us move toward this goal. The kids actually get this idea quickly in my classes. We review various situations and rewrite bad decisions into good decisions. The idea is to get the kids to stop worrying about things or situations they cannot control. Their focus needs to be on what they can control, which is their reaction.

Seeing the difference my class has had on my students and their parents has given me the inspiration to put my ideas into a book. The goal of my book is to help parents and kids reach a life that is full of inner peace and love so they can both achieve a higher self-esteem.

It is extremely rewarding to witness the kids in my class getting excited about the power high self-esteem can have in their lives. The greatest excitement occurs when the children are playing a game called Jeopardy. The game consists of two teams that are trying to answer self-esteem review questions. The winning team wins a prize. The kids are screaming out the answers with exuberance. Who would have thought a subject like self-esteem could get kids so excited.

Learning about self-esteem will make our children more confident. By learning how to improve our kids' lives, we will improve our own. We will learn there is an important link between our self-esteem and our children's self-esteem.

Discovering My Passion

It is rewarding to see our kids enjoying themselves. Seeing kids suffering mentally and being subject to ridicule is disturbing. Like most children growing up, I had moments of self-doubt. During my late teenage years, my father's alcoholism intensified. This caused my family much pain and suffering. Also during the same period, I had a major depression that was crippling. The depression caused great damage to my self-esteem and inner peace.

These events caused me to question what life was really all about. I began reading self-improvement books looking for answers. The more I learned about peace and happiness, the more philosophical and optimistic I became. Once I began mastering my own inner peace, I developed a burning desire to help others, especially children.

My goal is to help children avoid depression and low self-esteem. This is why I started my self-esteem program. I will provide advice based on my 15 years of teaching experience, 10 years coaching soccer and basketball, the experience of raising three sons, and my knowledge from reading over two-hundred self-improvement books.

Children – Life's Most Beautiful Flowers

We have to view our children as life's flowers. **<u>Children thrive and grow to their full glory when we give them love, respect, and kindness. When criticized, ridiculed, and abused, they wither and never reach their full height.</u>** Kids are too precious of a commodity not to be fully valued. I anticipate that you feel the same way or you would not be reading this book. Together we can make our society a better place by empowering our children, one child at a time.

Finally, I would like to conclude this section with my favorite poem, *The Most Beautiful Flower*. Author: Cheryl L. Costello-Forshey

The Most Beautiful Flower

The park bench was deserted as I sat down to read
Beneath the long, straggly branches of an old willow tree
Disillusioned by life with good reason to frown,
For the world was intent on dragging me down
And if that weren't enough to ruin my day,
A young boy out of breath approached me, all tired from
play
He stood right before me with his head tilted down
And said with great excitement, "Look what I found!"
In his hand was a flower, and what a pitiful sight,
With its petals all worn – not enough rain, or too little light.
Wanting him to take his dead flower and go off to play,
I faked a small smile and then shifted away.
But instead of retreating he sat next to my side
And placed the flower to his nose and declared with
overacted surprise,
"It sure smells pretty and it's beautiful, too.
That's why I picked it; here, it's for you."
The weed before me was dying or dead.
Not vibrant of colors, orange, yellow or red.
But I knew I must take it, or he might never leave.

So I reached for the flower, and replied, "Just what I need."
But instead of him placing the flower in my hand,
He held it midair without reason or plan.
It was then that I noticed for the very first time
That weed-toting boy could not see: he was blind.
I heard my voice quiver, tears shone like the sun
As I thanked him for picking the very best one.
"You're welcome," he smiled, and then ran off to play,
Unaware of the impact he'd had on my day.
I sat there and wondered how he managed to see
A self-pitying woman beneath an old willow tree.
How did he know of my self-indulged plight?
Perhaps from his heart, he'd been blessed with true sight.
Through the eyes of a blind child, at last I could see
The problem was not with the world; the problem was me.
And for all of those times I myself had been blind,
I vowed to see the beauty in life, and appreciate every second
that's mine.
And then I held that wilted flower up to my nose
And breathed in the fragrance of a beautiful rose
And smiled as I watched that young boy, another weed in
his hand
About to change the life, of an unsuspecting old man.

I read this poem to my students every year. It is a wonderful poem which fits very well with what I am trying to teach the children. The concept that our perception, or reaction, can change our world is the main idea in this beautiful poem. The old woman in the poem conveys this knowledge when at the end of the poem she states, "The problem was not with the world; the problem was me." The message learned here is not to look outside of yourself, but to know that control of your life has always been inside of you.

Teaching our kids to look within for guidance is the key. Blaming the world and our situation is not the way to go. To become a successful person, we just have to make the best decisions possible each day. By helping our children learn this vital skill, we can ensure they will have the best future.

PROLOGUE

IMPORTANT POINTS

1. Children with high self-esteem have good judgment and avoid negative consequences.

2. Life is all about choices. Children who have the gift of love see all the beauty in life and make wiser choices.

3. While we sometimes cannot change the situation, we will always have a choice in how we react to the situation.

4. Teaching kids to recognize negative choices, and replace them with better choices, is one of the keys to a life of inner peace and love.

5. Children thrive and grow to their full glory when we give them love, respect, and kindness. When criticized, ridiculed, and abused, they wither and never reach their full height.

THE PEACE PERSPECTIVE

A Book of Inspiration

Increase Your Child's Self-Esteem
by Helping Them to Discover a Peace Within

MIKE MARKOVSKI

Table of Contents

CHAPTER ONE
PEACE AND SELF-ESTEEM – THE LINK TO SUCCESS 5
   The Foundation 5
   The Key To Decision Making 7
   The Root Cause of Success 10

CHAPTER TWO
IT ALL STARTS WITH OUR PEACE PERSPECTIVE 17
   Our Peace and Self-Esteem Are Key 17
   The Importance of Our Inner Peace To Effective Living
   18
   Inner Peace And High Self-Esteem Starts At Home 25
   Let Children Know They Are Loved 26

CHAPTER THREE
HOW TO MAKE CHILDREN FEEL IMPORTANT 33
   Let's Put Children First 33
   The Importance of Listening To Children 35
   Help Children Avoid Attention-Seeking Behaviors 37
   Make Children Feel Special – Unconditional Love 41

CHAPTER FOUR
PEACE – A BETTER APPROACH TO LIFE 49
   Peace vs. Happiness 49
   Who We Really Are 53
   Creating A New Perspective 55
   Our Essence – Powerful and Constant 56

CHAPTER FIVE
A PEACEFUL MIND - CALM AND ALERT 63
   Meditation – Finding The Quiet In Life 63
   Mindfulness – Becoming More Aware 65
   The Now – The Present Before Us 67

The Violinist 68
Observe More And Think Less 70

CHAPTER SIX
HELPING CHILDREN SUCCEED 77
    The Power of Decisions 77
    Helping Children Find Their Passion And Purpose 78
    Setting Achievable Goals For A Lifetime Of Success ... 80
    The Importance of Believing In Yourself! 83

CHAPTER SEVEN
SOCIETY -- CREATING A NEW AND BETTER WORLD 89
    Bullying And Drugs: Threats To Our Kids' Well-Being
.... 89
    Our Schools – What Is Their Role? 91
    Advance Society With Our Own Inner Peace 93

EPILOGUE 99
APPENDIX 102

CHAPTER ONE
PEACE AND SELF-ESTEEM –
THE LINK TO SUCCESS

The Foundation

As parents, we have an awesome responsibility in raising successful, happy children. This responsibility is the most important task that we will face in our lives. Before we can succeed in this important endeavor, we need to understand the importance of what self-esteem is and why it is a key to our children's success. The simple definition of self-esteem is how you feel about yourself. How children feel about themselves will strongly influence the amount of success they have in their lives. There is no greater gift that we can give our children than the ability to have an unshakable confidence within. When kids learn to like themselves at an early age, they develop the confidence to succeed in life.

In order for children to really like themselves and know their true value, they must first discover a peace within. Understanding their value goes beyond their physical appearance. They need to know about their spiritual essence so they can discover their greatness. By basing their worth on their essence, they gain a greater sense of inner peace. A higher self-esteem arises with this new sense of inner peace. By fully realizing their own worth or greatness, they can approach life with more self-confidence.

As parents, we are our children's most important teachers. Our guidance, love, and support are what our children need in order to develop the confidence to face the life challenges that await them. **<u>How can liking ourselves and having inner peace be so important? These qualities are the key ingredients needed to raise positive children.</u>** Our focus, as parents, should be to provide these key ingredients to our kids so they can succeed in today's fast changing world. The problem is that some of us did not come from positive households. Therefore, one of our first tasks will be to learn to be more positive ourselves so that our kids can model our behavior. We will cover this topic in more detail in the next chapter.

The three main points to understand so far are: 1) High self-esteem is a great indicator of future success. 2) There is a link between inner peace and high self-esteem. 3) High self-esteem starts with positive parents and a positive home environment. Once we understand these points, we are on our way to helping our kids attain high self-esteem and inner peace.

The Key To Decision Making

In order to succeed in today's world, our kids will need a deep inner confidence. This confidence comes from their deep liking of who they are. With loving parents, our children can more easily obtain high self-esteem. An inner peace and love lifestyle (high self-esteem) is necessary because our kids are living in a world that has many problems. How they react to these problems and stresses will greatly determine their quality of life. Kids who do not have the gift of inner peace and love (high self-esteem) are, in a sense, left defenseless against a sometimes hostile world. Society has paid a price, including drugs, depression, crime and abortion, for our kids' lack of inner peace and love (low self-esteem). The main reason these problems occur is because some children are making bad choices. **The key reason bad choices occur is because some kids do not really like themselves. In other words, they have a low level of inner peace and love (low self-esteem).**

Both kids and adults with low levels of self-esteem cause many of today's problems. One of the best ways to make the world a better place is by removing low self-esteem. A key point to understand is that an individual's low self-esteem creates negative energy. This negative energy can cause us to make bad decisions. The decisions we make each day determine the quality of life we create for ourselves. Once we establish a high self-esteem, by increasing our inner peace, our decision-making improves. In essence, we are giving children the tools to succeed. By having a high sense of inner peace and love (high self-esteem), our children increase their positive energy. This positive energy is then all our children can give to the world.

We need to understand the importance inner peace and love have upon the way we interpret and react to life. For example, let us view our children's self-esteem as a force field that surrounds them. Our children have mostly a positive self-esteem force field or mostly a negative self-esteem force field. It is important to understand that there is a self-esteem range between low and high self-esteem. The closer our self-esteem is toward the highest range, the more effectively we deal with life. The opposite holds true for the negative end of the self-esteem spectrum range.

What does this all mean and what does this have to do with our children's happiness? The force field represents the amount of inner peace and control our children have upon their surroundings. Deep down, we all are searching for a sense of control in this ever-changing life. If someone can show us how to get this control, life could be lived in a much more effective way. By having high self-esteem, we obtain the peace and control to make good life decisions.

How is this possible? By the simple act of liking ourselves and believing that our essence is inner peace and love, we release a tremendous amount of positive energy within. This positive energy, once released, affects our confidence. A higher confidence gives us more fortitude and perspective to overcome most of life's difficulties.

An important point to understand is that we, at all times, cannot control all our situations. What we can control is our reaction to our situations. If we make good decisions, in most situations, we can live life at its highest level. Effective living should be the goal of each person. We must emphasize to our kids to focus only on what we can control, which is always our reaction.

Teaching our kids to have high self-esteem through inner peace and love increases their chances of making good decisions. The following is a very important clarifying point regarding the use of the force field, as we discussed earlier. This force field acts like a filter processing our life situations. **Each situation reveals our best course of action. This is only possible if we have a good self-esteem force field (perspective).** Therefore, by having good self-esteem, the proper decisions are more easily available to our children.

Another benefit of having a good self-esteem force field is that we are able to accept all of life's positive aspects. By having a good self-esteem force field, we believe and accept positive comments. We do not disregard them. People who have a negative self-esteem force field, most often, cannot accept positive feedback. Their force field acts like a shield that partially blocks positive feedback. A good self-esteem force field reveals the proper decisions to us. It also allows us to accept all the good life has to offer.

The Root Cause of Success

Our job as a society is to help our children to love themselves. When children have love, they see, more consistently, the beauty of life. Life is really a mirror of how we see ourselves. Dale Carnegie, one of the founding fathers of positive thinking, put it best with the following quote: "We are nothing more than what we think about all day long." **When our kids think about love, beauty, and peace, they draw these qualities to themselves.** The human potential movement has uncovered one basic defining principal: What we think about, and the images we hold in our minds, greatly influences the quality of life we lead. A person having a high self-esteem fits perfectly with this idea. People with high self-esteem hold positive images and expectations in their minds. These positive images and expectations from the inner self go outward and have a chance to become a reality. Many motivational thinkers believe we draw to ourselves the qualities we have inside of us. I believe people are like magnets. They draw like particles or qualities to themselves. That being the case, the importance of good quality thinking is more vital than ever.

To finalize the importance of the power of thought, note the following simple experiment: Dr. Judd Blaslotto, at the University of Chicago, conducted a study in 1996, where he divided a group of people into three groups. He tested each group on how many free throws they could make with a basketball. After this, he had the first group practice free throws every day for an hour. The second group just **visualized** themselves making **all** their free throws. The third group did nothing. After 30 days, he tested the groups again. The first group, who practiced shooting free throws every day for an hour, improved by 24%. **The second group, who just visualized making free throws, improved by 23% without touching a basketball!** The third group, who did nothing, did not improve at all, which was expected.

How could this be? The group that never physically shot any free throws in practice, but only visualized shooting perfect shots, got similar results as the group that practiced every day for a month. One explanation is that the visualizing group, by seeing success on every single shot, drew that result to a reality. The point of the study illustrates the power positive visualization has in our lives. This is why our tasks, as parents, are so important. By showing our kids the power of good thinking, we really can create the world we want! To achieve this, we first must create a better world inside of ourselves.

We may have "missed the boat" on trying to help solve our kids' problems. We mainly have been focusing our efforts and money on all the outcomes of poor self-esteem such as drugs, depression, violence, anger, etc. Our focus instead should be on the **root cause** of these outcomes, which is poor self-esteem or the lack of inner peace and love. By correcting the root cause of the problem, negative outcomes do not have a chance to manifest. Poor self-esteem is costing our society billions of dollars. Correcting the root cause of our problems would maximize the use of society's time, money, and energy.

To contain problems, we need to correct them before they spread to other areas of our lives. The first step to correcting a problem is awareness. We need to be aware that low self-esteem leads to most of the problems we see in the world today.

Society has not put enough focus and money toward finding ways for our kids to be more peaceful and to feel more loved. We all know that our kids are our most important resource. Our schools can be doing more in regards to increasing children's self-esteem. Schools need to make high self-esteem more of a focus in their curriculum. With parents and schools working together, we greatly increase our kids' chances for peaceful and fulfilling lives.

Is there anything more important than seeing our children become the best they can be? Children who love themselves do not turn into bullies, drug addicts, and criminals. Children who love themselves will not be disrespectful to others. **Children who love themselves can only give to the world what is inside of them - LOVE.**

CHAPTER ONE

IMPORTANT POINTS

1. How can liking ourselves and having inner peace be so important? These qualities are the key ingredients needed to raise positive children.

2. The key reason bad choices occur is because some kids do not really like themselves. In other words, they have a low level of inner peace and love (low self-esteem).

3. Each situation reveals our best course of action. This is only possible if we have a good self-esteem force field (perspective).

4. When our kids think about love, beauty, and peace, they draw these qualities to themselves.

5. Children who love themselves can only give to the world what is inside of themselves - **LOVE.**

WORDS OF WISDOM

There are no shortcuts to any place worth going.
~Beverly Sills

We must be the change we wish to see in the world.
~Mahatma Gandhi

The world never puts a price on you higher than the one you put on yourself.
~Sonja Henie

Real integrity stays in place whether the test is adversity or prosperity.
~Charles Swindoll

PARENTAL ADVICE

If love isn't taught in the home, it is difficult to learn anywhere else.
~Unknown

CHAPTER TWO

IT ALL STARTS WITH OUR PEACE PERSPECTIVE

Our Peace and Self-Esteem Are Key

Now that we know the importance of self-esteem, how can we help our children achieve a high self-esteem lifestyle? Fortunately, we play a vital part in determining our kids' level of self-esteem. To give our kids the best chance for success, we need to be the example. Kids are like sponges. They absorb all the behavior around them. We have an awesome responsibility to teach our kids how to react properly to life's many situations. Our children are modeling our behavior. By being strong role models, we can create a foundation of peace and love for our children.

There are many stories of children overcoming tough upbringings to become great successes. These stories get a lot of media play and are the exception rather than the rule. To ensure that our kids have the best chance for success, our lives need to be in order. Our positive role modeling will make good behavior feel natural for our children.

How do we model the best behavior for our children? This is a deep question with no easy answer. Like everything we have discussed, the answer starts with our own inner peace. **Our ability to have an inner calm and peacefulness are qualities of much value. In order to share these qualities with our kids, we need to possess them first.**

The Importance of Our Inner Peace To Effective Living

Since having an inner peace and loving lifestyle is so important to successful living, you would think that it would be one of the most pursued qualities in life. If we all had this quality, generation after generation of parents could pass inner peace and love to their kids. This really is the easiest way to learn – role models showing us a successful way to live. Sadly, this has not been the case throughout history. In fact, the opposite has been occurring. Parents have been passing on to their kids various coping techniques as ways to deal with life. While some coping styles are more effective than others are, most coping styles are not at the highest level our kids deserve.

Why are most parents failing to give their kids the best tools needed to reach their maximum potential? Most parents never had this inner peace and loving lifestyle modeled to them by their own parents. For centuries, parents did the best they could. Parents simply gave their kids the best advice they knew. I am not blaming parents in any way for their parenting styles. People, in general, do the best they can with what information they have available to them.

Luckily, over the past 50 years, the interest in positive thinking has exploded. More people want to reach a peaceful state. They are attending seminars and reading books on how to live lives that are more peaceful. While this is very encouraging for our society, the percentage of people living a lifestyle of inner peace and love is still too low. We need to show people how to become more peaceful so they can start embracing the calm within.

As I mentioned before, I have spent much of my own life asking some deep questions about life. I had serious self-doubts when I was a teenager. I had bouts of sadness that caused me much suffering. I started to question many things about life. I wanted to know what life was about. What makes people happy? What is inner peace? How did life begin? While the discussion for most of these questions is for another book, the discussion of inner peace is very relevant here. My point is that because of my own struggles, I have some ideas that could help you and your children achieve greater inner peace. My search for inner peace has been instrumental in the writing of this book.

At this point, I would like to focus on one key point of inner peace since this is a very deep topic. The key point is to shift people's focus from chasing happiness to seeking inner peace. It is vital to understand the main difference between peace and happiness. Peace is constant and internal. Peace is not fleeting and external like happiness. Happiness mostly comes from things outside of us like family, friends, possessions, money, love, etc. These things, obviously, are very important to our well-being. However, since these things are outside of us, we cannot control them. By not being able to control these things, happiness can come and go. Therefore, happiness is not a constant event.

Peace, on the other hand, is very different. Peace is internal. It comes from the knowledge that we, as individuals, are very powerful beings. Our power comes from our inner awakening to the miracle of life. This miracle gives each person the power to think, to love, to have a body, to have a soul, etc. Our essence, which is extremely powerful, is the source for our well-being. **By realizing our essence is peace and love, we release the tremendous energy inside of ourselves. We awaken to our real self, which is pure peace (essence), and not our ego (body).** This new realization increases our consciousness. The increased consciousness then gives us more control of our lives.

Life has a direct connection with our essence. Our false identification with the ego separates us from our connection with life. Our essence connection causes us to see life from a higher perspective. We realize that we cannot control things outside of ourselves. We rely on something that we can control at all times, which is our sense of inner peace and our reaction to whatever situations life presents us. Control is the main thing we are looking for in life. Inner peace gives us this control. While we cannot always control the situation, we can always have control of our inner peace. By controlling our inner peace, we can have better control of how we react to life.

Getting kids and parents to believe they have ultimate control over their lives has been the focus of my class and this book. Power from within can only come when we know our essence is pure inner peace and love. With this knowledge, peace enters our lives. Once we accept full responsibility for how we feel, we cannot blame others for how we do feel. People often take the easy way out. They blame life's situations for how they are feeling. It is so much easier to blame the world than to accept responsibility for our feelings.

We often rely on other people or situations to dictate how we feel. This causes us to have feelings that fluctuate with each situation we encounter. Things outside of us now control our feelings. Once this happens, we can claim we are a helpless victim. We are then not responsible for our feelings. We give up control, not only of our feelings but also, of our lives. The reason I am telling you this is so you can learn how to achieve inner control so you can find more peace within. How can we help our kids if we are showing them that we are a victim? How can we preach for self-reliance and self-love in others, if it is not within ourselves?

No magical formula exists that will give us a life that is filled with constant peace. Inner peace is possible, but only, if we believe we can achieve it. The quickest way to achieve inner peace is by simply accepting you are pure love and not the ego. Our perspective changes with this new understanding. We achieve more inner peace knowing we are part of the whole of life (love) and not separate from life (ego). This knowledge allows us to gain more peace within, which then reflects in our everyday lives.

What does it mean to live as the whole of life (love) and not separate from life (ego)? What does this look like in our daily life? The key aspect to any idea or theory is its ability to affect our lives. Can the idea or theory make a difference in our so-called "reality"? I have personally experienced the two forms of perspective; varying emotions and a constant inner peace and love. Therefore, this is really my view on how a change to a higher perspective (inner peace and love) can change our world.

When we begin to see ourselves more as a spirit or essence, we notice changes within ourselves. Our outer world has not changed, but our perception of our world has changed. By realizing we are part of the whole of life, we stop struggling. We stop trying to prove our worth to others and ourselves. We now understand we are not weak or separate from life, but we are connected and central to life's very existence. Our essence is the foundation for our worth. This understanding reveals to us how beautiful, powerful, and eternal we are. A peaceful aura surrounds us as we now go about our daily life. We enjoy life much more. We make better decisions at every turn.

To live in this new way, we will first need a new understanding in our lives. This understanding develops our ability to live knowing our true essence in each moment. This is where most people fail. The vital awareness of their true essence in each moment is not consistent so their inner peace comes and goes. Since we have not trained ourselves to keep this awareness (peaceful aura) around us, consistently, we sadly believe this inner peace life is simply not attainable. By practicing mental discipline, we can master the ability to live life as the essence and not the ego.

The best reaction to any situation will reveal itself to the person who has an inner peace within. Staying calm, looking for the best options, having a confident outlook, knowing our worth and seeing a positive outcome, are all signs of a person with a peaceful aura. Handling life with peace, dignity, and compassion should be the goal of all people. Life is full of change. There is so much beauty in life and, unfortunately, opportunity for much stress. We can best deal with it all by mastering our ability to face the world with our true essence. This should be the guiding principal in how we react to life.

The guiding principal to our reactions should be our inner peace and love (essence**). We need to buy into the idea that our reactions, not our situations, create our feelings.** This is good news because we actually can control our reactions, but we cannot always control our situations. Our inner peace reaction is the one thing we have absolute control of in life. There is great comfort in realizing this. We now have something constant in our lives that we can always hold onto.

By acquiring a sense of inner peace and love, we can learn to react positively to any situation. We can take back control of our lives. Just by being aware of this new kind of understanding, our life changes dramatically. We stop blaming others because this is no longer our way. Instead of blaming the world, we start living! We learn to make the best of any situation. We learn to release things we cannot control.

We need to master these techniques before we can pass them on to our kids. There is no better tool for effective living than knowing that our peace resides within. If there is nothing else you learn from this book, please make it this: **OUR REACTION, NOT THE SITUATION, DETERMINES OUR DESTINY!**

Inner Peace And High Self-Esteem Starts At Home

We need to be positive role models for our kids. Our actions are of the highest importance when it comes to leaving lasting impressions. Showing our children how to live life in an effective way can help them to live a more successful life. When we react to life in a loving way, it makes a real difference because kids see a positive way that can work for them. Most kids have a hard time overcoming poor parenting. Make your kids' success as easy as possible. Show them daily proper life reactions. Your modeling can make all the difference!

We must make sure our kids associate with friends that have inner peace and high self-esteem. It is more difficult to raise positive kids when they associate with friends who lack inner peace and love and are motivated solely by external events. **Our children's poor choices of friends will diminish our efforts of modeling peaceful behavior.** Parents make a crucial mistake by not monitoring the character of each of their kids' friends. Although it is natural that people influence our children, we must realize how much of this influence can be negative and damaging to their lives.

Other negative factors could also cause difficulties for our children. The first area to monitor is other people in our kids' lives, besides their friends. These other people, which may be a negative factor, include relatives, neighbors, and classmates. The second area, which may not be as obvious to us, is the media. By the media, I mean television, the Internet, video games, books, magazines, radio and social media. Negative information can enter our children's lives in so many ways. Consistently watching violence on television or playing violent games can fill our kids' minds with negatives images. We need to limit their exposure to these negative sources. With less negative images, our kids can begin to see all the beauty around them.

Modeling good self-esteem and removing negative factors are great ways to help our kids become more peaceful. We need to surround our children with peace in the home and beyond. By creating a loving environment, we are helping our children have a better chance for a more successful life.

Let Children Know They Are Loved

What is another way we can help our kids on their life journey? We must let our kids know how we feel about them every day. It should not be a secret that we love and respect our kids. We should tell our children "I love you" at various times of the day. It does not have to be unnatural to do this. Yet, this simple act of love is not as common as it should be. This is likely because we did not receive this simple expression of love from our parents when we were kids.

Many people are not comfortable saying "I love you" to others because it feels unnatural to them. Most likely, these people came from homes that never believed in expressing love in words or actions. If this is the case with you, then the change will need to start with you. Do not keep your love locked up inside. We should share our love with the people we love. Our expression of love will help those we care about know, without a doubt, how special they are to us.

I came from a home that did not express love in words. I made it a point not to let this continue when I had a family. Ever since our children were born, my wife and I have made it a point to tell our sons, several times a day, that we love them. Having children participate in this exchange can be a challenge in itself. Our sons have found it natural to respond with "love you" when we express our love to them.

Another sign of affection we need to convey to our kids is through the giving of hugs. This physical touch between human beings is so very important. This physical touch backs up the expression of love we say to each other. A study carried out in the late 1950's confirms the importance of touch in all living beings. Harry Harlow, American psychologist, conducted a series of experiments with infant rhesus monkeys and a set of "surrogate mothers." The two main types of "mothers" used were *a wire model containing a bottle to feed the monkey and a terry-cloth model.* Despite the fact that the baby monkeys only received food from the wire mother, all of the monkeys spent more time clinging to and cuddling with the terry-cloth mother, especially when they were frightened. This disproved the prominent "cupboard theory," in which it was believed that infants only had an attachment to their mothers because they were the source of food, thus associating the mother with positive feelings. The baby rhesus monkeys' attachment to the cloth mothers led researchers to conclude that attachment and the need for affection was deeper than the need for food. This study illustrates the importance of contact between living beings.

Make it a habit to hug your kids on a regular basis. For example, when our kids were small, in addition to their many hugs during the day, we would give them what we called a "one minute hug" before they went to bed. Although we called it a "one minute hug," the time always lasted much longer. It was a time for our kids to share with us what they were feeling. They expressed their feelings while we laid in bed next to them, hugging them and talking about their day. This time was an expression of love that we all enjoyed. These were moments we looked forward to each day.

Everyone needs to look for ways to convey their affection to each other within their family structure. Our embrace could be the warmth our kids are seeking in a sometimes very cold and impersonal world. Our kids might tell us that it is not cool to get hugged or to get emotional. Deep down, I think this is just a cover. **We all need signs of affection. This need is what makes us so unique. It is something we never outgrow.** A parent's love is a great sense of comfort for their children. Kids need to know that their home is a safe area for them to escape from life's pressures. Our job is to make our home a place where our kids come for comfort and answers. The world needs to love its kids unconditionally because they are our most treasured resources. Children who are loved will return their love back into the world in many ways.

CHAPTER TWO

IMPORTANT POINTS

1. Our ability to have an inner calm and peacefulness are qualities of much value. In order to share these qualities with our kids, we need to possess them first.

2. By realizing our essence is peace and love, we release the tremendous energy inside of ourselves. We awaken to our real self, which is pure peace (essence) and not our ego (body).

3. We need to buy into the idea that our reactions, not our situations, create our feelings.

4. Our children's poor choices of friends will diminish our efforts of modeling peaceful behavior.

5. We all need signs of affection. This need is what makes us so unique. It is something we never outgrow.

WORDS OF WISDOM

There are two ways of meeting difficulties: you alter the difficulties, or alter yourself to meet them.
~Phyllis Bottome

Success does not come to you ... you go to it.
~Marva Collings

The ultimate measure of a man is not where he stands in moments of comfort but where he stands at challenge and controversy.
~Martin Luther King Jr

For myself, I am an optimist – it does not seem to be much use being anything else.
~Winston Churchill

PARENTAL ADVICE

I am my child's most important teacher.
~Unknown

CHAPTER THREE

HOW TO MAKE CHILDREN FEEL IMPORTANT

Let's Put Children First

Our time is valuable so how we allocate that time reveals what we value. It seems as though life is a constant juggling act. One of our greatest challenges is to keep everything organized. Life is moving at a faster pace than ever before. We are struggling to keep up. What does this fast-paced lifestyle have to do with our kids' self-esteem? Parents have to decide how they will distribute their time as it becomes more precious. In order for our kids to have high self-esteem, they need our time. If we cannot find the time for them, they will be the first to notice. Children, most of the time, are not going to verbalize this need. We have to recognize their need for our time so we can give them the love and attention they deserve. Once we notice their need for our time, we can find ways to provide for it. When kids feel loved, they have more of a chance to do great things. This is why we need to find ways to give our time and love to our kids. Words alone will not make them feel important. **When we start**

making plans for our time, we need to first start with our kids in mind. Our loving attention is the most important gift we can give our kids.

As my sons were growing up, my wife and I set specific times where our children were our sole focus. We called this time together "family time." Several times a week, during the evening, we would get everyone together. We would have an open forum. This was our time to share our feelings and bond. Our children, at first, complained because they did not see the need for this so-called "family time." After a while, they began to welcome family time. There were countless times where we went over our thirty-minute time limit. These moments together were a time when any one of us could share our thoughts, hopes, and fears. We have reminded our children that there is no excuse for not finding some time for your family daily. Your family should get together at whatever intervals work for them.

To develop a level of trust with our kids, we must start earning that trust at an early age. When our kids believe and trust us, they learn to share their feelings more often with us. This is important because they will turn to us when they have problems or concerns. Once our kids come to us for answers, we can help them select the best path possible. If our kids shut us out, they will go elsewhere for answers. By giving our kids more loving attention, they will realize that we are their best source for guidance when problems arise.

Putting our kids first, by giving them our time, can help them trust us. It can also help them understand how important they are to us. Making our kids our top priority is the best investment of our time we can make.

The Importance of Listening To Children

Most parents are good at telling their kids what to do. We have no problem informing our kids when they make bad decisions. We also have a habit of bypassing our kids' good news. Then, we often end up spending too much time on the bad news. Do we really know how to listen to our children? By listening to them with real interest, we can help make them feel special. We can make our children feel special by getting excited and showing some emotion when we hear good news from them. We need to show our children just how proud we are of them. By asking for details and showing genuine interest, we convey to them they are important to us.

There are a couple of key points to keep in mind when listening to our kids. First, as we would expect of them, we should not interrupt them when they are talking. We should let them finish before we offer them advice or feedback. We should ask for clarification but keep our advice or feedback to ourselves until we get the full story. When we do offer our advice, we should keep in mind our kids' feedback. In the end, we should let our children make their own decisions as often as possible. By making their own decisions, they learn valuable life skills. The other point to keep in mind is, when listening, we must not be critical. We must not be too harsh when our kids make mistakes. Real growth can happen when children do not fear making mistakes. They will learn that their mistakes are correctable. We are there to offer guidance and support. We are not there to yell at them. Yelling at them will make them feel inferior. We must point out our kids' mistakes in a supportive manner so they can learn from their experiences. We must guide them so they can provide their own solutions and options. This way, our kids can develop their problem-solving skills. **When our kids know we will be kind and supportive, especially when they make mistakes, they will come to us for guidance.**

Getting our kids to talk to us when they have problems is probably one of the most important steps toward helping our children achieve a higher self-esteem. By being good listeners, we can gain our kids' trust. They will want to come to us and share their feelings. By gaining our kids' trust, they will come to us at all times, even when they have bad news.

Help Children Avoid Attention-Seeking Behaviors

Kids who feel loved have less of a need to increase their self-worth through attention-seeking behaviors. Kids who feel loved and valued usually have high self-esteem. They feel secure in who they are. They have less of a need to prove their worth to the outside world. By knowing their essence, they can find a constant sense of worth. They value their own opinion, more than the opinion of others. This is a very important trait to possess because it allows our kids to control what they think of themselves. Control is very important. Having control within means we can change how we feel. We are not overly dependent on what other people think of us to feel worthy. This increased sense of inner dependence will make a child more confident within, without the need for frequent outside approval.

One of the problems in today's society is that some kids are lacking loving support as their foundation from their parents. If a loving foundation is not available at home, they will search for a loving foundation elsewhere to support their worth. Parents need to be there for their kids, consistently and continuously, to shape their kids' foundation of self-worth. If not, outside forces may become a more dominant presence in shaping their children's self-image. Often times, unfortunately, these outside forces are a poor substitute.

Acceptance becomes more crucial for external-seeking or ego-centered kids. Their worth becomes more dependent on outside acceptance. Ego-centered children will go to great lengths to gain acceptance by the outside world.

An example of this kind of needed acceptance would be kids gaining attention by radically changing their body appearance. Kids change their appearance because they are seeking attention to increase their sense of self-worth. They get odd haircuts, hair colors, tattoos, and piercings on different parts of their bodies. These attention-seeking actions occur so people will notice them. These kids are saying, "Hey, look at me! I need attention! I will go to any means necessary to get your attention."

Why has attention-seeking behavior been increasing recently in our society? Children not being able to find an inner peace and love within has led to the recent increase in attention-seeking behavior. Kids have used attention-seeking behaviors to gain the attention and love that is missing in their lives. Being noticed and loved is one of our greatest needs as human beings. Children will not allow others to ignore them. When children feel ignored, the attention they yearn for can lead to negative behavior. This negative behavior is acceptable for most of these ego-centered kids. They feel some attention, caused by the negative behavior, is better than no attention at all.

The need for negative attention can sometimes escalate. Less serious issues, like tattoos, can become more serious. These children can suddenly face issues like drugs, alcohol, and criminal activity. Kids will sometimes resort to these activities if they feel unloved by their parents and others. By pursuing negative activities, kids are actually crying out for help. They are begging their parents to take notice of them. Having others appreciate us is very important. It is one of our greatest human needs. Kids can get confused in how to get our attention. Some of these kids will resort to getting attention in the only way they know when they are feeling hurt. They turn the hurt they feel inside of themselves onto the outside world by displaying negative behavior.

You must be wondering what is so important about our children's attention-seeking behavior. When children receive recognition, it means that they are receiving attention. We all need the feeling of being recognized. However, there is less of a need to look for attention when we have good internal qualities. Having good personal internal qualities like integrity, honesty, compassion, kindness, and peacefulness means we have high self-esteem. By being a person of high character, our real inner peace and loving self can emerge. Our foundation of high self-worth leads us toward living a peaceful life largely independent of outside negative influences.

As we know, children with a deep inner belief in themselves can accomplish great things. This is because children with high self-esteem have good decision-making habits. These good decision-making habits are the key to effective living. **<u>Kids who cherish themselves for their internal values do not need to look beyond themselves to discover who they are. They will not base their worth on what others think of them.</u>** These inner peace and loving kids live a high quality life. We need to move our kids away from external-based, attention-seeking behavior. Our kids' positive worth should not be based upon society's acceptance of them. A positive worth is created only by their own belief in who they are - a peaceful and loving essence.

Kids whose behavior is determined by a lifestyle of inner peace and love can only release positive energy into the world. Positive energy is all that is inside of them. Once these inner self-guided kids obtain inner peace and love, outside forces will not easily influence them. These kids now have a clearer direction in their lives. Children with goals have a clear vision in which to make their dreams become a reality. Inner self-guided kids know what they want. They will not listen to discouraging words. Inner self-guided kids will focus on finding ways to get through life's rough patches. They have a vision of what is important to them. These inner self-guided kids will not only get what they want, but will do so in a loving manner.

As parents, we have a clear mission. We must help our kids find their inner peace and love within.

Again, to achieve this state, we must absolutely believe that our essence is inner peace and love. By believing in our powerful essence, we release the tremendous power within our consciousness. Our reactions now come from a higher perspective because of this new awareness of our higher consciousness. The best option in each situation is now magically more evident. We cannot have negative behavior or reactions when we have mostly inner peace and love within. By realizing this new approach to life, we will improve both our inner and outer world!

Make Children Feel Special – Unconditional Love

Conveying how we feel can sometimes be difficult. It seems much easier for us to convey to our kids, and others, our frustrations rather than our appreciation. This does not seem right, but this is how society functions. We can see this as being true by simply watching how some young children treat each other. Kids, starting in early elementary school, make fun of kids who look and act different. It is not very often we see kids complimenting each other. This trend continues in many ways into our adult lives. This kind of behavior is a reflection of how we treat ourselves.

Unkind behavior occurs because we are living an ego-centered life. Our life is not one of inner peace and love. We learn at an early age to focus on our areas of perceived flaws. Therefore, our focus is seldom on our areas of strengths. We are tough judges when it comes to ourselves. This reflects in how we behave toward our world. It is very difficult to feel special when we are mostly looking at our perceived flaws and discounting our good points.

For some strange reason, we have accepted an ego-centered life as normal. Living an ego-centered lifestyle is causing our society to live below its full potential. This ego-centered lifestyle starts at an early age for most of us. I really think it all starts with parents. Unknowingly, because of a concern for our kids' safety, parents become overly protective. When our children are babies, we are constantly watching them so we can help them avoid trouble. In other words, we catch our kids doing things wrong. Of course, this is for our children's own protection. The problem is parents set a pattern for themselves, and for their kids, that conditions their behavior. We set a pattern of catching our kids doing things wrong. We learn to notice the bad behavior rather than the good behavior. In order to make our kids feel special, we need to turn this around. **We need to start noticing and catching our kids doing things right.** Ken Blanchard, motivational author, introduced and promoted this idea to the world.

When my children were young, my wife and I gave them a point for every time we caught them doing things right. These points turned into a small monetary payoff based on their point total for that month. By giving our kids' good behavior a reward, they learned that we appreciate their good behavior.

Catching our kids doing things right is very important to their self-confidence. Equally important is the parents' ability to properly correct the child's behavior when it is negative. We must always distinguish between the bad behavior and the child itself. By correcting the child's behavior, we are not questioning or challenging their worth. We are saying we are just upset at their behavior and not at them. Children can change a behavior easier when they know their parents still love them. Our love can help our children learn that they are still special, even when they make mistakes.

Children need to know they will receive unconditional love no matter what. They also need to know they have parents, or people in their lives, who will always love them. There is nothing more special than knowing that we do not have to earn our parents' love. Our parents' love is constant in a world full of change. This love is always there and it does not come and go. Unfortunately, in today's world, too many parents only provide love with conditions. There should be no conditions placed on the love we give to our children.

Some kids feel they have to battle to earn their parents' love. This puts a lot of pressure on these kids to perform in a certain manner. For example, a child can believe unless I get straight A's...unless I make the basketball or cheer team...etc., I know my parents will not love me. If this is true, it is a sad testimony to the state of our world. Our kids should not have to struggle to earn what should be there at all times – our love. Getting our kids to believe in our unconditional love can be a challenging task. There are not many examples of unconditional love for them to experience. Most societies believe that in order to receive something, we must earn it first. Of course, it is important to expect full effort from our children. How can we blame children who give full effort? Children can always control their effort but they cannot control the result of this effort. When our children know they have our love, no matter what the result of their full effort is, this can mean everything to them!

It is important for our kids to know they are always special to us. Once they know they have our love, they will not continue to struggle in trying to earn it. We will need to show our love to our kids every day, consistently. No matter whether our kids' behaviors are good or bad, we must offer the same amount of love. Obviously, if this behavior is bad, we will correct the behavior with advice, firmness, love, and compassion. If the behavior is good, we need to make a big deal about it. We need to tell our children, more often, how proud we are of them. **<u>Our kids need to see a consistent love from us, no matter how they behave. With a consistent love, they will believe in the existence of an unconditional love.</u>**

Human beings have a deep emotional need for love that is central to our survival. If this love goes unfulfilled, it could lead to possible destructive behavior. Our number one goal, as parents, is to instill this feeling of inner peace and love within our children. First, we must help our kids believe their essence is one of inner peace and love. Then, we need to convey each day to our kids that we love them unconditionally. This way, our kids will not feel pressured into thinking they have to be perfect, or act only in a certain way, to gain our love.

Making our children feel special is one of the most important things we will ever do in our lives. When our children feel special, there is no limit to what they can accomplish. An unconditional love will allow our children to be themselves. They will know they do not have to be perfect to receive our love. Our constant love can be their guide to a fulfilling life. For our love to have a full impact, we need to give our kids more than encouraging words. We will need to give them a love full of emotion. Continuously and consistently, we need to show our kids the affection they deserve!

CHAPTER THREE

IMPORTANT POINTS

1. When we start making plans for our time, we need to first start with our kids in mind. Our loving attention is the most important gift we can give our kids.

2. When our kids know we will be kind and supportive, especially when they make a mistake, they will come to us for guidance.

3. Kids who cherish themselves for their internal values do not need to look beyond themselves to discover who they are. They will not base their worth on what others think of them.

4. We need to start noticing and catching our kids doing things right.

5. Our kids need to see a consistent love from us, no matter how they behave. With a consistent love, they will believe in the existence of an unconditional love.

WORDS OF WISDOM

When we cannot find contentment in ourselves, it is useless to seek it elsewhere.
~La Rochefoucauld

Success requires three bones ... wishbone, backbone, funnybone.
~Kobi Yamada

The height of your accomplishments will equal the depth of your convictions.
~William F. Scolavino

A happy person is not a person in a certain set of circumstances, but rather a person with a certain set of attitudes.
~Hugh Downs

PARENTAL ADVICE

Children want their parents' attention and will go to extreme lengths to get it.
~Unknown

CHAPTER FOUR

PEACE – A BETTER APPROACH TO LIFE

Peace vs. Happiness

The previous chapters were important in establishing a base for understanding the importance of self-esteem. Those previous chapters were building blocks so you would appreciate the importance of self-esteem and the role you play in your children's quality of life. In this chapter, we are narrowing our focus. We will be getting into specific ways to achieve the quality of life we all want for our kids. In the next two chapters, we will be discussing several techniques that will help our kids reach the peace they deserve.

Let us start by expanding on the topic we discussed in Chapter 2, PEACE. Understanding that we need to base our lives on the foundation of peace, and not happiness, is a key first step. Our inner peace and love is significant to awakening the inner peace and love within our kids.

There are no magical cures to make life's problems go away. However, there are steps to make life more understandable and more fulfilling. No matter what path our kids are currently on, they can improve their lives in some way. Although people have all kinds of different needs, deep down, we all have the same basic need for attaining a sense of inner peace and love within. The misunderstanding of this basic human need is why society has not reached its most peaceful state of existence. Most people continue to look for answers outside of themselves (happiness) instead of within (peace). Let us explore this issue more in depth so we can clarify this misunderstanding.

Why do people want money, health, love, kids, etc.? The typical answer given by most people is the happiness these life aspirations provide them. These life aspirations are a means to an end. The feeling of happiness, these life aspirations provide, is what most experts believe we are all seeking. Let us look at one of our pursuits as an example. The reason we pursue money is that we believe it will eventually provide us with happiness. Why do we work? Because, we know, the money we earn will allow us to buy food and pay for our living expenses. In addition, we can save some of the money we earn for our retirement. While these needs are essential to our survival, money is still a means to an end. We want money for the things it can eventually provide us. Earning money and acquiring things gives us the feeling of happiness. Most people in life are looking for feelings of happiness. They are willing to put up with pain, in the short term, knowing, in the long term, that this pain will eventually provide them with feelings of happiness.

This is important to understand because we want to know what is the most important quality we, as human beings, are chasing? Once we know this, we can discover ways to achieve it in the fastest way possible. We also want these feelings of happiness for our kids. We, as parents, want to convince our kids that we can help them achieve these feelings of happiness. What person or kid does not want help in achieving happiness in the fastest way possible?

If you remember, most experts believe that we are all seeking these feelings of happiness. I believe there is something deeper and more rewarding than happiness. What feelings can be deeper than happiness? Peace within is our greatest human need. **<u>Our feelings of happiness are fleeting emotions that are not stable or constant. Peace provides us with the constant and stable feelings we are seeking.</u>** Peace is the natural state out of which we came into this world. Somewhere along the way, we have lost that natural essence of who and what we are. Our true purpose is to regain this important quality in order to live at our highest means.

Why is pursuing a state of peace more important than pursuing a state of happiness? A state of happiness exists in the external world. The state of peace is an internal experience. We reach a state of peace by knowing that our essence is inner peace and love. By understanding this idea, we can influence our children's lives to the highest degree. To live a peaceful existence, we need to understand our true nature so we can learn to control our feelings. Why is this so important? The increased control of our feelings leads to a greater control of our behavior. A greater control of our behavior leads us to a higher quality of life.

How do happiness and peace come into the equation? How we deal with controlling our feelings dictates how we see and react to life. In a pursuit of happiness approach to life, outside factors control our feelings. We do not fully control our feelings. Our feelings occur because of what is happening all around us. This is the normal process for most people. The inner peace and love lifestyle, while not common, is much more effective in dealing with life. **The inner peace and love lifestyle does not focus on the events around us. Our focus is not on what is occurring but on how we react to these events.** The focus is on our inner self (our self-talk) rather than external events (occurring life events).

While this all may seem confusing, the essence of understanding it all is simple. The important task of controlling our feelings is through either the internal (peace) lifestyle or the external (happiness) lifestyle. Of course, life events will naturally cause an array of feelings within us. Good or bad events will automatically cause corresponding feelings within us. This is normal and the way life is lived by most people (happiness lifestyle). To get to a higher level, we have to learn to live the peace lifestyle.

What do I mean by this? We need to develop the ability to stay in a constant zone of peace so we have better control of our feelings. In this constant zone of peace, we maintain a higher state of consciousness so we can more effectively monitor how we talk to ourselves.

Who We Really Are

How do we maintain this higher consciousness form of living? The answer lies in a very simple concept that, if mastered, can unlock a higher lifestyle for us all. We can unlock this concept with the simple act of visualizing and really believing in our true nature. This new belief will allow us to enter and stay, more frequently, within the zone of peace that is so liberating.

To achieve a higher consciousness, we need to remove our faulty self-image. By seeing ourselves as a separate body and ego, we end up viewing life with a very limited perspective. To access the tremendous power source within us, we need to see ourselves in a very new way. **By changing how we see ourselves, we change our perspective**. Our new perspective changes how we react to our world. As Deepak Chopra, renowned spiritual author, stated so eloquently, "We are not just a drop of water in the ocean, but instead, we are the entire ocean." **By seeing our essence connected to the whole of life and not just to ourselves, we transform our perceptions and our world.**

I know what you must be thinking. While this information is philosophical and interesting, it has no implications for me in my daily life. We need to believe, however, that by changing our perspective of who we really are, we greatly influence our moments. We cannot react in fear when we realize, in that moment, we are at our essence inner peace and love. The negative energy in our world occurs because we have forgotten our true nature. By forgetting our true nature, we react as the ego and not as our true essence, which is love. To live in peace, we just have to master our ability to see ourselves as who we really are in each moment, more consistently. To make it all possible, we have to believe in our own greatness and in the greatness of others. To maintain this new awareness of our true essence, we will need to develop our ability to monitor our thinking. By controlling our self-image and our thinking, we can begin to control both the world around us and within us.

Creating A New Perspective

Most people are not very aware of what they are saying to themselves. In fact, various studies indicate that most of the things we say to ourselves are negative in nature. Our thoughts are also very repetitive. To improve our thinking, we need to raise our awareness level. This will allow us to be more conscious of what we are saying to ourselves. By thinking more effectively, we can live a more fulfilling life.

In reaching a new level of peaceful attention, we can understand that the peaceful way of processing our world is much more effective in living a higher quality life. Let me give you a simple example that I use in my self-esteem class. As we discussed previously in this book, we have two students facing the same situation. They have a test coming up. The student with the happiness lifestyle approach will view this as a stressful situation. This happiness approach, which is more ego-based, produces a lower consciousness level. This lower consciousness causes the student to be less aware of the various thoughts he is processing. Being unaware of his negative thoughts creates doubt within. This leads to feelings of anxiety, which reduces his chances for success. The student with the inner peace and love approach is more conscious of his thinking. He has a connection to his essence of inner peace and love. This child is more aware of what he is saying to himself. He is more able to correct his thinking. To have success on the test, he needs to be in control of his thinking and his feelings. This child says positive things like "I know I will do well on the test," or "I believe in myself." This inner dialogue produces good feelings. This child is also more relaxed. While this is a simple situation, we can see how far-reaching this new approach can have on life. Reducing stress by making better decisions, through a more peaceful state, is the key to living a more peaceful life.

Our Essence – Powerful and Constant

Once our children understand the source of power that is within them, they will not be lacking in self-confidence ever again. I am not talking here of a boastful ego-centered existence. A boastful ego-centered existence comes from a person with a low self-esteem outlook. In the ego-centered life, we do not fully love or like ourselves. We try to convince others how good we are because deep down we do not believe in our own self-worth. Unfortunately, too many people live these ego-centered kinds of lifestyles. They are busy trying to convince themselves, through various ego-centered actions (chasing prestige, money, fame, etc.), that these activities will increase their sense of worth. Their essence is ego-based. Peace is not central in their lives. While it is necessary to strive for the activities mentioned above, they do not really fulfill us deep inside. These ego-centered actions continuously leave people unfulfilled in life. Because these things are not constant and controllable, they do not provide us with the peace we are seeking.

What is constant and controllable? Our peaceful essence is constant and controllable. Our essence is inner peace and love, which is naturally very powerful and intelligent. We just need someone to remind us of the special qualities we are all born with. We need to show our kids how to appreciate the special qualities that they have inside of themselves. The fact that we can control and maintain our bodies, the fact that we can think and be aware of all that is around us, and the fact that we were born and are even here to experience life, we often take all this for granted. Amazingly, we never really think about the specialness of all these events.

We have not properly conveyed to our kids to appreciate the power that guides their lives. There is less of a need to prove ourselves (less ego) when we know the power that we all have inside of us. Our worth comes from the knowledge that we are a "peaceful essence." Our power lies in recognizing how we, as our essence, can control our body, mind, and perception. **Our essence is the most powerful force in the universe**. However, this power can only be unleashed if we acknowledge it and, more importantly, believe that this is who we are. This knowledge will inspire our lives and make us realize that our worth is constant. There is really no need to prove our worth to anyone. To be a human being is a special privilege. The earlier we get our children to appreciate their bodies, minds, and spirits, the more peaceful their world will be.

A big problem with our society is that we have a tremendous need to prove ourselves. We spend most of our lives trying to prove that we are important. We spend our lives trying to convince ourselves and others that we are someone who should be valued. Once again, we do this because we are living an ego-centered life, which is about acquiring and seeking. It is also about proving our worth. We try to accumulate material wealth and prestige to show others that we have achieved a certain level of status. We spend most of our lives trying to squeeze as many activities into our lives as possible. We act as if we are going to win an award by accomplishing more than anyone else accomplishes. We do this because one of our greatest needs is to be recognized. We want to know, and we want others to know, that we are important.

What if there was a different approach where we never have to question our worth? No matter what we have accomplished in life, our self-worth would remain of high value. We do not have to prove our self-worth to anyone. This is such a liberating way to see the world! I do not think one person's life is more worthy than another person's life. On the surface, people have different levels of achievement. An extreme example would be a homeless person's life in comparison to the President of the United States' life. While their achievements may be at the opposite end of the spectrum, their essence and their self-worth are the same.

We have to value each person's life equally, if we want to view life in the proper perspective. This perspective maintains that our essence, which is inner peace and love, makes us all the same. We are beyond judgment from anyone. Our actions do not determine or change our worth. We cannot look at a person's life and judge them only on their life's accomplishments. We must see life from a perspective that each individual is like an actor playing a part in a play. We all have parts in this play of life. Our roles cannot dictate the worth of our essence, which is constant and of the highest value.

We must show our children that their internal worth is unchanging and of the highest value. Children do not have to battle for any outside acknowledgement that they have tremendous value. They can see themselves as worthy from their birth. **Our worth is innate. We do not have to struggle for it. With this understanding comes a peace and love that is awe-inspiring.**

To reach our natural essence of inner peace and love, we must simply accept that we are peace and love. With this new understanding, we replace our lower-conscious thinking. Lower-consciousness thinking causes us to be more ego-centered. Ego-centered thinking causes us to be separate from the whole of life.

For help in mastering our inner peace and love awareness, we need to explore the practices of meditation and mindfulness. These practices increase the mind's concentration so we can better control our consciousness.

CHAPTER FOUR

IMPORTANT POINTS

1. Our feelings of happiness are fleeting emotions that are not stable or constant. Peace provides us with the constant and stable feelings we are seeking.

2. The inner peace and love lifestyle does not focus on the events around us. Our focus is not on what is occurring but on how we react to these events.

3. By seeing our essence connected to the whole of life and not just to ourselves, we transform our perceptions and our world.

4. In reaching a new level of peaceful attention, we can understand that the peaceful way of processing our world is much more effective in living a higher quality life.

5. Our worth is innate. We do not have to struggle for it. With this understanding comes a peace and love that is awe-inspiring.

WORDS OF WISDOM

The superior man blames himself. The inferior man blames others.
~Don Shula

What lies ahead of you and what lies behind you is nothing compared to what lies within you.
~Mohandas K. Gandhi

Destiny is not a matter of chance; it is a matter of choice.
~Unknown

Do not follow where the path may lead. Go instead where there is no path and leave a trail.
~Unknown

PARENTAL ADVICE

If your child feels safe, wanted, and loved – you are a successful parent.
~Unknown

CHAPTER FIVE

A PEACEFUL MIND - CALM AND ALERT

Meditation – Finding The Quiet In Life

In recent years, many people in our Western culture have discovered the power meditation has in reducing stress. While this approach is new to America, it has been around for thousands of years in the Eastern cultures of China, Japan, and India. The idea of meditation is actually quite simple; quiet the mind from the constant chatter.

The Western mind is always thinking and looking for constant stimulus. It cannot seem to slow down. Most people feel like they have lost their ability to control their minds fully. Their minds are actually controlling them. Many people say they cannot stop thinking for any length of time. They have never done it. They really do not know how to stop the constant mind chatter.

Meditation gives the mind a chance to relax. This allows the mind to reset itself. By slowing down our mind, we can increase its performance. People are always looking for ways to deal with stress. Not only does meditation increase our mind's focus, but it also has the added benefit of reducing our stress level. There is a reduction in our stress level because, during meditation, we try to eliminate much of our thinking. When we have no thoughts, we cannot have any stress.

Why is there no stress when we have no thoughts? In order to have stress, we have to be thinking about a situation irrationally. Irrational thinking creates our problems because we are not thinking about our problems in the best possible way. If we have no thinking, we cannot have any chance of irrational thinking. Our stressful situation may still exist, but we are no longer aware of it. This knowledge will help us to reduce the stress in our lives.

There are many different ways to achieving a meditative state. Do some basic research to find a style that works best for you and your child. The technique you choose should include deep breathing, silence, and a releasing of thoughts as they enter your consciousness. I would recommend a starting meditative interval of once a day for ten to fifteen minutes in the morning or just before bedtime. You will need to discover a time and place that works for you. **The important thing to get out of meditation is the ability to relax and quiet our**

<u>minds. By doing this, we get more control of our minds and thus more control of our thinking.</u> This increased control of our thoughts will lead to a more peaceful existence.

Mindfulness – Becoming More Aware

Mindfulness is a technique in which you are very aware of each moment. The goal of mindfulness is to take that meditative calm state of being into our everyday lives. We can achieve a mindfulness state of being only by first understanding what gets us out of our calm state. Irrational thinking creates the negative emotions we have in our lives. Although emotions are important because they give life to our feelings, we need to make sure we do not allow needless mental suffering to dominate our thinking. By removing irrational thinking from our minds, we can enjoy our emotions fully without the unnecessary anguish in our lives. One way we can reduce our mental suffering is by significantly reducing or turning off our constant thinking throughout the day.

How can we function without thinking? We do not have to eliminate thinking, but we can reduce our thinking by up to eighty percent. As I mentioned earlier, various studies indicate that our thinking is mostly negative and redundant. We mostly say the same negative things to ourselves day after day. We create emotional pain through our irrational thinking and negative words. Often, we are unaware of what we are really saying to ourselves. We are on autopilot and we enter a trance-like state where our awareness level is very low. This lower level of awareness is what causes us to miss the many negative things we say to ourselves.

Our minds typically wander. This wandering causes our minds to spend too much time in the past or future moments. This drifting of the mind creates problems. When we think about the past, we usually focus on how things should have been different. We have guilt for something that we did not do or could have done better. Those things have already occurred. Thinking about them does not change our present situation. We are wasting our time by thinking about the past in this way. On the other hand, when we think about the future, we are usually planning or worrying about some unpleasant upcoming events. By spending too much time in the past or the future, we create guilt and worry within ourselves. **Guilt and worry only cause us to waste our energy. We can remove both guilt and worry by simply staying in our now moments.**

Of course, we can think of positive events when we reflect about our past or look forward to events in the future. These kinds of reflections, outside of the now, are enjoyable. They are an essential part of our everyday experiences and we should value them. However, living too often in the past or the future will cause us to miss the beauty of the present moment.

The Now – The Present Before Us

The vividness of life is only available in the clarity of the current moment. When we are present with our consciousness, we learn to fully appreciate our now moments. While we can enjoy the past and look forward to the future, we must learn to live more fully and consistently in the now. Living in the now, more consistently, allows us a better way to control the future. By being present, we create more awareness within.

No changes can occur in the past since the past is gone. The future can only change with the decisions we make in the now. We need to treasure the gift of the present by being alert and focused. We can never remove ourselves from the now. This is where our decisions affect the life situations we encounter. To have a clearer course in life, we must be focused and alert. Like a light dimmer switch, we can face the now with a dim level of awareness or a high level of awareness. The amount of brightness (consciousness) we confront life with will determine our decisions and the quality of the life we lead. The choice has always been with us. Now, we can see that we have the power to dial up our brightness (consciousness) so we can make our lives more peaceful. Also, with our brightness turned up, we can more easily see all the beauty life has to offer.

The following story illustrates how so many of us miss the beauty that is all around us each day.

The Violinist

A man sat at a metro station in Washington DC and started to play the violin; it was a cold January morning. He played six Bach pieces for about 45 minutes. During that time, since it was rush hour, it was calculated that thousands of people went through the station, most of them on their way to work.

Three minutes went by and a middle-aged man noticed there was musician playing. He slowed his pace and stopped for a few seconds and then hurried up to meet his schedule.

A minute later, the violinist received his first dollar tip: a woman threw the money in the till and without stopping continued to walk.

A few minutes later, someone leaned against the wall to listen to him, but the man looked at his watch and started to walk again. Clearly, he was late for work.

The one who paid the most attention was a three-year old boy. His mother tagged him along, hurried but the kid stopped to look at the violinist. Finally, the mother pushed hard and the child continued to walk turning his head all the time. This action was repeated by several other children. All the parents, without exception, forced them to move on.

In the 45 minutes the musician played, only six people stopped and stayed for a while. About 20 gave him money but continued to walk their normal pace. He collected $32. When he finished playing and silence took over, no one noticed it. No one applauded, nor was there any recognition.

No one knew this but the violinist was Joshua Bell, one of the best musicians in the world. He played one of the most intricate pieces ever written with a violin worth $3.5 million dollars.

Two days before his playing in the subway, Joshua Bell sold out at a theater in Boston and the seats average cost was $100.

This is a real story. Joshua Bell playing incognito in the metro station was organized by the Washington Post as part of a social experiment about perception, taste and priorities of people. The outlines were in a commonplace environment at an inappropriate hour: Do we perceive beauty? Do we stop to appreciate it? Do we recognize the talent in an unexpected context?

One of the possible conclusions from this experience could be:

If we do not have a moment to stop and listen to one of the best musicians in the world playing the best music ever written, how many other things are we missing?

Huffington Post, Washington Post 2/15/09, 11/17/11

Observe More And Think Less

As *The Violinist* illustrates, we are missing the many miracles of life. What is causing us to miss the beauty that is all around us? We are failing to be fully conscious of each moment before us. People are rushing constantly from one moment to the next. We do not stay present enough in each moment to absorb fully all that life is offering us. We have conditioned ourselves to perceive each moment outside of the present moment as being more valuable. **The common perception seems to be that there is something always better than what is in front of us. This is an illusion that causes our lives to feel unfulfilled.** We must realize that everything we value in life is in front of us. We just need to stop and soak in the moments fully. Our lives do not have to change for us to appreciate the moments before us. All it takes is an awakening of our inner being. To achieve an awakened state, we need to learn how to gain control of our minds. With this awakening, we come to our senses and everything slows down. We become more alive and live more in the moment.

The benefits to our inner world can be dramatic with this new higher state of awareness. Our inability to control our consciousness creates many of our problems. By disciplining our minds, we can experience life with a better perspective. With a disciplined consciousness, our inner world becomes suddenly more peaceful.

How can we keep this higher state of awareness for longer periods? As we discussed earlier, the secret lies in developing our focus to be more consistently engaged. The "chatter" in our minds causes our consciousness to be scattered and unfocused. By controlling our minds, we can absorb our moments more fully. We now become the moment. The difference between watching a moment and becoming the moment is like night and day. When we are the moment, we are getting all the energy from it. When we are watching the moment, we are getting only a small portion of that energy. When we are the moment, we are connected or "in the zone" during this special time. We do not have to settle for these special moments as uncontrollable events. We can learn to master our minds so we can have more of these peak periods as a regular part of our lives.

Everyone can learn to master the power within. The mindfulness technique I have been describing is simple to master. The key to using the mindfulness technique is the ability to "observe more and think less." When we are thinking, we are not present with our consciousness. Therefore, we miss the experience before us to some degree. We have a habit of either worrying about something in the past or fearing something in the future. Thinking is very important but only when it is productive. **By observing our now moments fully, we become the experience. We absorb the experience and get full value from the moment.** We all have had the experience of having dinner and not remembering how the food tasted. We were not present and we missed the experience. Our consciousness was not there. It was elsewhere thinking, talking, etc. We miss a large portion of our life because we are not present with our consciousness.

Why are people still living at a lower level of existence? Most people simply have not awakened to their vast potential. By realizing our true essence and living mindfully, we can create a higher existence. People today, especially kids, cannot be still for very long. They need multiple experiences to keep themselves entertained. With mindfulness, we can do routine tasks and get more out of each experience. Various routine tasks, such as cooking, cleaning, playing, and even doing homework, can actually be enjoyable when done mindfully. When we observe and are present fully, we are in our natural state of peacefulness.

I know what we have been discussing can be difficult to understand. Thinking is a way of life for most people. People have a very difficult time turning off the mental chatter. We need to change our life direction by getting back to our natural essence. Our natural essence is to observe our world free of any judgment.

CHAPTER FIVE

IMPORTANT POINTS

1. The important thing to get out of meditation is the ability to relax and quiet our minds. By doing this, we get more control of our minds and thus more control of our thinking.

2. Guilt and worry only cause us to waste our energy. We can remove both guilt and worry by simply staying in our now moments.

3. The vividness of life is only available in the clarity of the current moment. When we are present with our consciousness, we learn to fully appreciate our now moments.

4. The common perception seems to be that there is something always better than what is in front of us. This is an illusion that causes our lives to feel unfulfilled.

5. By observing our now moments fully, we become the experience. We absorb the experience and get full value from the moment.

WORDS OF WISDOM

When a man is wrapped up in himself he makes a pretty small package.
~John Ruskin

The true value of a human being is determined primarily by how he has obtained liberation from the self.
~Albert Einstein

It is a dangerous thing to ask why someone else has been given so much. It is humbling – and indeed healthy– to ask why you have been given so much.
~Condoleezza Rice

Being defeated is often a temporary condition. Giving up is what makes it permanent.
~Marilyn vos Savant

PARENTAL ADVICE

At the end of the day, the most overwhelming key to a child's success is the positive involvement of parents.
~Jane D. Hull

CHAPTER SIX

HELPING CHILDREN
SUCCEED

The Power of Decisions

How do we reach a natural, peaceful state? The answer lies in something we do just about every moment we are living which is make choices. How can the simple act of making a choice be a crucial part in providing peace and direction to our lives? The power of choice determines our life direction. There is a direct link between making quality decisions and a high quality life. **We can make better decisions by reaching our natural state.** Life becomes much easier and our choices become more self-evident once we reach our higher level of awareness.

We can react to a situation in a positive manner or a negative manner. Like a driver who comes to a fork in a road, we must decide what course our car will take. Everything we encounter, from this point, occurs because of the previous turns (decisions) we made. Similarly, we change our life course based on the decisions (turns) we select. This is why selecting a positive course is vital to living a highly peaceful life. The more times we make the right decisions (turns), the more life rewards us with the life we have envisioned.

Many spiritual thinkers believe our new natural state of consciousness acts like a GPS (Global Positioning System) dictating our course to a more enriching life. These guiding universal signals lead us in choosing the right path. These signals have always been there for humanity. God, or the universal consciousness, has provided us with guided directions. They are only available to us when we are at our highest frequency or consciousness.

By removing our ego, we can reach a higher state of consciousness. While this may seem very philosophical, the message is simple: Life rewards us when we live our lives with a universal-focused mindset rather than an ego-focused mindset. We can see ourselves as insignificant, as the ego, or we can see ourselves, spiritually, as powerful and timeless.

Helping Children Find Their Passion And Purpose

What is the next step now that we have a new perspective and awakened children with the ability to make good sound decisions? We need to help our kids find what makes them passionate. This passion will become their life guide. Why is finding our children's passion so very important? Finding our children's passion will dictate the direction that makes our children's lives fulfilled. Many people do not know what they want out of life. This means most people have no clear path or life direction. The first thing a new company lays out for itself is its mission. The company clearly states the purpose for its existence. With a clear purpose, the employees can now work together, more effectively, to achieve the company's goals. Without clearly defined goals, all future employee actions become less productive.

People, like companies, need clear directions to achieve their life goals. A lack of life direction has left many people frustrated. Most people have never taken the time to find out what makes them passionate. They have not established their life goals. With life goals, we increase our chances for making our passions a reality. People who are fortunate enough to discover their passions live more fulfilling lives. People, who have passion and a state of peacefulness, spend their days moving toward their dreams. The same formula for a successful life keeps reappearing in the biographies of famous people. Most famous people found their passion at an early age. This passion provided them with a drive to succeed and overcome their obstacles.

Some people do not have a passion or clear life goals. Having no life clear goals would be like taking a plane, from Detroit to Chicago, but not putting in the coordinates. These people then wonder why their lives are not fulfilling. They also wonder why life has taken them on so many unexpected journeys.

We are all born with a dream or a passion. Some people are just more aware of what their dreams and passions are. One of our most important tasks is to discover what our dreams and passions are. We all have heard stories of young kids that become master painters, musicians, dancers, singers, etc. These kids became exceptional because their dreams and passions took over their lives at an early age. Their dreams and passions created the energy to make their aspirations come true.

To find where our kids' passions lie, we need to examine the kind of things they enjoy. These interests convey what our kids find exciting and what makes them feel good. From this knowledge, we can find a central passion that excites our kids and makes them come alive.

Setting Achievable Goals For A Lifetime Of Success

Some people make the mistake of thinking they must put their passion to the side when considering a career. They often look at future job growth projections to decide their career path. **When we**

are not determined to follow our passion, we settle for less than we deserve. If our life goals are not clear, other people will replace our dreams with their own dreams. We cannot afford to let this happen to our children. We need to let our kids know the importance of making their own dreams a reality.

Let us look at a particular example, such as a child who loves collecting baseball cards. How can a child make a career out of collecting baseball cards? This child could envision himself owning a sports memorabilia store. Once the child graduates from high school, he can attend college to obtain a degree in entrepreneurship. In addition, he can search for a highly successful businessperson, who has opened a similar store, to model. During this time, he could dedicate himself to becoming a top expert in collectibles. By doing all the above, a viable fulfilling career can become a reality.

To be at the top of any profession, we must have a passion within. We must not let our kids settle for a field that does not provide a chance for a passionate life. Children can learn that eventually they can make a living doing what they love! Sometimes, our kids just need some help in seeing all the possibilities. It takes some planning on the front side in order to help our children discover a fulfilling career. **We all want our kids to get the most out of life. To achieve a fulfilling career, they need to follow the passion in their hearts.**

Having a passionate career helps us achieve a passionate life. We all can have a fulfilling life, but only, when our goals are in line with our inner reality. When we are at peace, the direction of our life becomes easy to see. Our essence guides us toward the correct path. Suddenly, all aspects of our life fall into place. Our goals become more self-evident.

We have to be observant to what makes us feel fulfilled. Whether we are trying to build a fulfilling career or a happy family, the approach is the same: **LISTEN TO YOUR ESSENCE OF INNER PEACE AND LOVE**. The passion that is deep within us will guide us in the right direction.

Our life needs to be in balance so we do not lose sight of all that is important to us. A good example of a balanced life would be to think of the major parts of our lives as a wheel. Anthony Robbins, inspirational speaker and author, noted that several components comprised the so-called wheel of life.

1. Physical Body
2. Emotions & Meaning
3. Relationships
4. Time
5. Work/Career/Mission
6. Finances
7. Celebrate & Contribute: Spiritual Sense

When in equal balance, the wheel operates properly. However, most people are not in balance.

This imbalance distorts the roundness of the wheel. When our balance is lost, we cannot move efficiently through life with this unbalanced wheel. As Anthony Robbins discusses, this distortion of the wheel balance is determined by our varying level of attention in each area. To regain a more balanced wheel, we simply need to correct how much attention we give to each area. By having this life balance awareness, we will not allow any one part of our life to dominate the other parts.

The Importance of Believing In Yourself!

To achieve our goals, we will need a deep belief in ourselves. We must never doubt ourselves. If we do not have this strong belief in ourselves, then our chances for success will be severely limited.

How do we help our kids form a foundation of a deep belief within? The key lies in our kids having a high self-esteem through a sense of inner peace and love. Children who feel good about themselves can believe anything is possible. **With a belief in our own greatness, we can visualize the success that is within us.** We all know anything that is worthwhile will have obstacles, which will cause us to think about giving up. The bigger the goal, the bigger our obstacles can be. The ability to overcome these obstacles to success is the hallmark of successful people. The greater the belief we have in ourselves, the greater are our chances to overcome these bigger obstacles. Our children's confidence will dictate their level of success.

Sometimes the difference between success and failure can be very small. The people who usually succeed are the ones who go that extra mile. They keep trying just a little longer than everyone else does. We must teach our children to believe in themselves, without any doubts. Kids who believe in themselves, without any doubts, have a high persistence level. They do not give up. They view barriers as temporary. Their barriers will not stop them from achieving their goals. Their positive outlook will keep their minds working for solutions instead of giving up too soon.

Successful people do certain things well to achieve a high level of success. They leave clues for others to follow so they can achieve similar results. Life rewards people who continue to work toward their dreams. To illustrate this point, I have listed several amazing examples of successful people who overcame great obstacles to achieve success. The following information is from an article, *But They Never Gave Up*, found at the University of Kentucky website:

➤ **Inventor Thomas Edison** failed 1,000 times before he discovered the light bulb.
➤ **Renowned children's writer Dr. Seuss** had his first book, *To Think I Saw It on Mulberry Street*, rejected by 27 publishers.

- ➢ **Pulitzer Prize winning author Margret Mitchell** was rejected by 38 publishers for her award winning book, *Gone with the Wind*.
- ➢ **Business mogul Walt Disney** was fired by his newspaper editor for having "no imagination." He then went bankrupt several times before building Disneyland.
- ➢ **Physicist Albert Einstein** was described as "mentally slow" by one of his teachers. The world famous Zurich Polytechnic School would not admit Einstein as a student.
- ➢ **One of the greatest basketball players of all time, Michael Jordan,** failed to make his eighth-grade basketball team. Michael Jordan has stated that he missed over 9,000 shots and 26 game-winning shots during his career. His secret to success, "I failed over and over and over again in my life. That is why I succeed."

Most famous people have had to endure numerous rejections and failures before eventually succeeding. Imagine how much our world would have lost if these great people gave up too soon. They confidently persisted toward their vision against overwhelming obstacles. Now, imagine all the people who have actually given up before reaching their own vision. These people never shared their dreams with the world. What a great loss for humanity. This is why teaching our kids to be very determined is so vital to our world.

Most people naturally focus on negative outcomes instead of positive outcomes. They defeat themselves before they even take the first step and try. A strong belief in ourselves will allow us to maintain confidence when things look bleak. We need to remind our kids to believe in themselves. In this way, we can ensure they have the best chance for success. By believing in their essence of inner peace and love, our children can have the energy needed to overcome any life obstacle.

CHAPTER SIX

IMPORTANT POINTS

1. Many spiritual thinkers believe our new natural state of consciousness acts like a GPS (Global Positioning System) dictating our course to a more enriching life.

2. To find where our kids' passions lie, we need to examine the kind of things they enjoy. These interests convey what our kids find exciting and what makes them feel good.

3. When we are not determined to follow our passion, we settle for less than we deserve. If our life goals are not clear, other people will replace our dreams with their own dreams.

4. We all want our kids to get the most out of life. To achieve a fulfilling career, they need to follow the passion in their hearts.

5. With a belief in our own greatness, we can visualize the success that is within us.

WORDS OF WISDOM

Winners expect to win in advance. Life is a self-fulfilling prophecy.
~Unknown

Success is a journey, not a destination.
~Winston Churchill-

What the mind of man can conceive and believe, the mind of man can achieve.
~Napoleon Hill-

Our greatest glory is not in never falling, but in rising every time we fall.
~Confucius-

PARENTAL ADVICE

Children need hugs more than things.
~Unknown

CHAPTER SEVEN

SOCIETY – CREATING A NEW AND BETTER WORLD

Bullying And Drugs: Threats To Our Kids' Well-Being

Why do we have the problem of bullying? We have to understand that bullies are children that have negative energy within. Certain situations trigger the release of their negative energy into the world. This negative energy results in put-downs, anger, and meanness to others. Bullies do not really like themselves. This is why they try to hurt others. Bullies want to put others down so they can feel superior. Bullies make themselves feel better by making others feel worse.

We want our kids to feel good so they can give positive energy to other children. Our children need to be ready to handle bullies when, and if, bullies ever confront them. Having high self-esteem allows kids to block out the negative messages the bullies are conveying. High self-esteem kids do not allow negative talk to control them. They believe in themselves and continue on their positive path, no matter what obstacles they encounter. **It is very dangerous when our kids believe the negative messages they hear. The energy and passion diminishes within our children when they believe these negative messages.**

Schools are beginning to realize fully the devastating effects bullying can have on students. Some schools are trying to implement bully-free zones. Unfortunately, bullying, at its worst, can lead to kids taking their lives. This very serious issue is finally getting the attention it deserves. The bullies themselves need special attention. These kids are crying out for help. Their low self-esteem is causing the self-hatred that is so harmful to themselves and others. With special attention, these kids can realize there is a better way. Bullies need intense classes on inner peace and love to awaken the love within.

Another concern we have for our kids is drugs and alcohol. There is a simple reason people use drugs and alcohol. They are trying to change how they feel. Most are struggling to escape boredom or some painful aspect in their lives. People abuse drugs and alcohol because they have poor thinking patterns. They are looking for something outside of themselves to solve their current problem. This is a recipe for trouble. When we give up control of our lives, we will not find the peace we are looking for. The drug and alcohol problem has continued to escalate. Our world has not learned to look within for answers. Drug and alcohol abuse will never be an option for children who have a firm control of their thinking.

Deep down, all kids and adults have good natures. By giving love to our kids, we can help awaken this deep self-love within. Children who have learned to be responsible for their feelings will not look outside of themselves for answers. We are beginning to see, no matter what the problem, the answer is always the same: **Reacting correctly, with our peaceful essence, to our life situations**!

Our Schools — What Is Their Role?

Having more self-esteem classes in elementary schools would show our kids that a peaceful and loving life is possible. At this crucial age, children would get help in understanding how beautiful and powerful they really are. We need to let our schools know that our communities need more self-esteem classes. These classes would help show our kids how much inner peace and love they have. An inner peace and loving lifestyle is vital to solving many of the issues our world is facing. Finding ways to help our children reach their full potential is vital for our society.

Our first priority should be to assemble additional task forces. Their job would be to examine the feasibility of making this inner peace lifestyle a reality for our children. A key target age to teach kids the value of high self-esteem is between the ages of 8 to 12. Kids at this vulnerable stage of life are establishing their boundaries. They are learning all about themselves. Their ego-centered life often focuses on perceived body imperfections. Their image suffers as they have unrealistic expectations of how they should look and feel. These unrealistic expectations cause children to have low self-esteem. These kids have not learned to be accepting of themselves. Children mistakenly think they are the only ones having doubt and confusion about who they are. Self-esteem classes would teach our children that what they are going through is normal. This will help them feel less isolated and confused.

Children need to understand how powerful they are! People can say many bad things to them, but they have the ultimate power. This is where their real power resides—inside themselves. **Nobody can make children feel inferior without their permission. We never want them to believe they are anything but beautiful, powerful, and intelligent.** Through regular self-esteem classes, our schools can help in making this belief a reality!

We can help raise our kids properly now or pay billions of dollars in the future to correct the damage caused by our children's negative self-esteem. It is madness not to correct a problem at its source, which is the negative thinking inside our children. We have the power to correct bullying, drugs, violence, and self-hatred now, before these problems have a chance to start.

Advance Society With Our Own Inner Peace

The world can become a better place, but only if we change from the inside out. We have made such significant advances, especially during the last century. Physically, we have made our lives easier, but what about our spiritual advancement? The following poem, *The Paradox of Time*, explores this issue further.

The Paradox of Time

The paradox of time in history is that we:
Have taller buildings, but shorter tempers
Wider freeways, but narrower viewpoints
We spend more, but we have less
We buy more, but enjoy it less

We have bigger houses and smaller families
Bigger churches and smaller congregations
A multitude of prayers but very little faith
A blessed life, but lack of gratitude
A loving God for our blemished hearts

We have more conveniences, but less time
We have more degrees, but less sense

More knowledge, but less judgment
More experts, but more problems
More medicine, but less wellness

We have multiplied our possessions,
But reduced our values
We talk too much, love too seldom, and hate too often
We have learned how to make a living, but not a life
We added years to our life, not life to our years

We have been all the way to the moon and back
But we have trouble crossing the street to meet a new neighbor
We have conquered outer space, but not inner space
We've cleaned up the air, but polluted the soul
We have split the atom, but not our prejudice

We have higher incomes, but lower morals
We have become long on quantity, but short on quality

These are the times of tall men, and short character
Steep profits and shallow relationships
More leisure, but less fun
More kinds of food, but less nutrition
These are the times of two incomes, but more divorce
Of fancier houses, but broken homes

It is a time where there is much in the show window
And nothing in the stock room
A time when technology can bring this letter to you

And a time when you can choose to make a difference
Or just hit delete

By Dr. Bob Moorehead

Humanity's values need to change as *The Paradox of Time* eloquently illustrates. Over the last century, we have made our lives so much easier, at least from a technological point of view. These changes, however, have not made our lives more peaceful. As the poem emphasizes, our values have not kept up with our material wealth. Just how much wealth do we really need? In order to have more fulfillment, we need to decide what we value the most in our lives.

When our society begins to place more value on inner peace and love over "things," we will see both our inner world and outer world transform. The last century has been a transformation of our outer world (technological advancements). This century we will begin to transform our inner world (spiritual advancement) at a more rapid rate than ever before. With this spiritual advancement, the values *The Paradox of Time* questions will be corrected.

Now, because of our continual spiritual growth, we will visit that new neighbor, remove our prejudice, and not pollute our souls. With a new commitment to our spiritual growth, the things we value spiritually can truly be ours. This path will not be easy because humanity has been on a path between awakening and darkness throughout its history. Some estimates have shown that in the last century, one-hundred and sixty million people died due to wars between humans. This same century also brought the greatest technological advancements ever seen by humanity. This contrasting human behavior has caused many people to question the sanity of our human race. We are a species that can advance itself to great heights or destroy itself. **Humanity needs to shift our focus and resources, more spiritually, in order to advance ourselves. We need to advance our inner dimensions before it is too late.**

CHAPTER SEVEN

IMPORTANT POINTS

1. It is very dangerous when our kids believe the negative messages they hear. The energy and passion diminishes within our children when they believe these negative messages.

2. Nobody can make children feel inferior without their permission. We never want them to believe they are anything but beautiful, powerful, and intelligent.

3. We can help raise our kids properly now or pay billions of dollars in the future to correct the damage caused by our children's negative self-esteem.

4. When our society begins to place more value on inner peace and love over "things," we will see both our inner world and outer world transform.

5. Humanity needs to shift our focus and resources, more spiritually, in order to advance ourselves. We need to advance our inner dimensions before it is too late.

WORDS OF WISDOM

Remember no one can make you feel inferior without your consent.
~Eleanor Roosevelt

The answer lies within ourselves. If we can't find peace and happiness there, it's not going to come from the outside.
~Unknown

Always give without remembering and always receive without forgetting.
~Brian Tracy

Life is too short to spend time with people who suck the happiness out of you.
~Unknown

PARENTAL ADVICE

You should treasure your children for what they are, not for what you want them to be.
~Unknown

EPILOGUE

The Peace Perspective — Changing Our World

As I discussed in the previous chapters, we have seen what negative energy can cause throughout history. There is no reason to think that an increase in positive energy, within each one of us, cannot create a better world where people see each other as more similar than different. We all have to see ourselves as connected by our essence or spirit.

The beauty of this shift to our higher consciousness is that we move away from our ego. An egocentric life is a limited view of the world. The inner peace life reveals the connection we have to all of life. We now have a greater need to help others due to our peaceful awareness. It has been said that when Jesus entered a room, he could raise the energy of the entire room. We can have the same effect but on a smaller scale. Once we harness the power within, we change our world.

Many skeptics believe a peaceful perspective for humanity is just not possible. Before historical changes can occur, there is usually great doubt that these changes could ever become a reality. Some ideas that seemed unrealistic were the earth being round, the sun being at the center of our galaxy, the discovery of electricity, and the invention of the computer. People believed these were all ideas that could never become a reality.

To make any great change, society needs visionary people to see a future that many others simply cannot possibly envision. Visionary people are the reason great inventions and change has occurred throughout history. Humanity is slowly waking up to its essence of inner peace and love. By removing our ignorance and increasing our consciousness, we can uncover our true peaceful nature. This "awakening" occurs at different times for each person. Some people are more ready than others to attain this natural level of consciousness.

Still many people have not awakened to a universal essence lifestyle. They are living an ego lifestyle because they just do not see any other way. People need help to raise their awareness level so they can see over their mental barriers to a better way. Our new lifestyle allows us to stop making bad decisions. It also allows us to create a life that is more fulfilling. Others will see our peaceful lifestyle and naturally will want a life that is more fulfilling.

While you and I never asked to change the world, it is something that comes about naturally. Just by living our lives in this new way, we change all that we touch. The negative source or ego, once removed, cannot produce the negative energy, which causes all our problems. To awaken the beautiful reality within, we just need a deep belief in who we are, which is peace and love. Our essence is the most beautiful and powerful force in the universe. By having an unshakable belief in who and what we really are, we can unlock the tremendous power that is deep within each one of us. We all can make our world a better place, but only if we live life with the peace perspective!

APPENDIX

Book Recommendations

Title / Author

Fifty Success Classics
Thomas Butler-Bowden

The Secret
Rhonda Byrne

The Success Principals
Jack Canfield

How To Win Friends & Influence People
Dale Carnegie

Book Of Secrets
Deepak Chopra

Getting The World You Want
Deepak Chopra

Life After Death
Deepak Chopra

Power, Freedom, and Grace
Deepak Chopra

Parenting Teenagers –STEP
Don Dinkmeyer, Sr /Don Dinkmeyer, Jr/ Gary D.
McKay/Joyce L. McKay

Change Your Thoughts – Change Your Life
Wayne Dyer

Excuses Begone!
Wayne Dyer

It Is Never Crowded Along The Extra Mile
Wayne Dyer

Power Of Intentions
Wayne Dyer

Ten Secrets For Success and Inner Peace
Wayne Dyer

Wisdom Of The Ages
Wayne Dyer

Never Be Average
Tim McCormick

A New Earth: Awakening To Your Life Purpose
Eckhart Tolle

Bringing Stillness Into Everyday Life
Eckhart Tolle

Entering The Now
Eckhart Tolle

Even The Sun Will Die
Eckhart Tolle

Gateways To Now
Eckhart Tolle

The Art Of Presence
Eckhart Tolle

The Power Of Now
Eckhart Tolle

Conversation With God
Neal Donald Walsh